Blossom

A FLORAL COLORING BOOK FOR RELAXATION, UNLEASH YOUR INNER CHILD, AND ENHANCE MINDFULNESS

by Joanna Williams

THIS COLORING BOOK BELONGS TO

_____

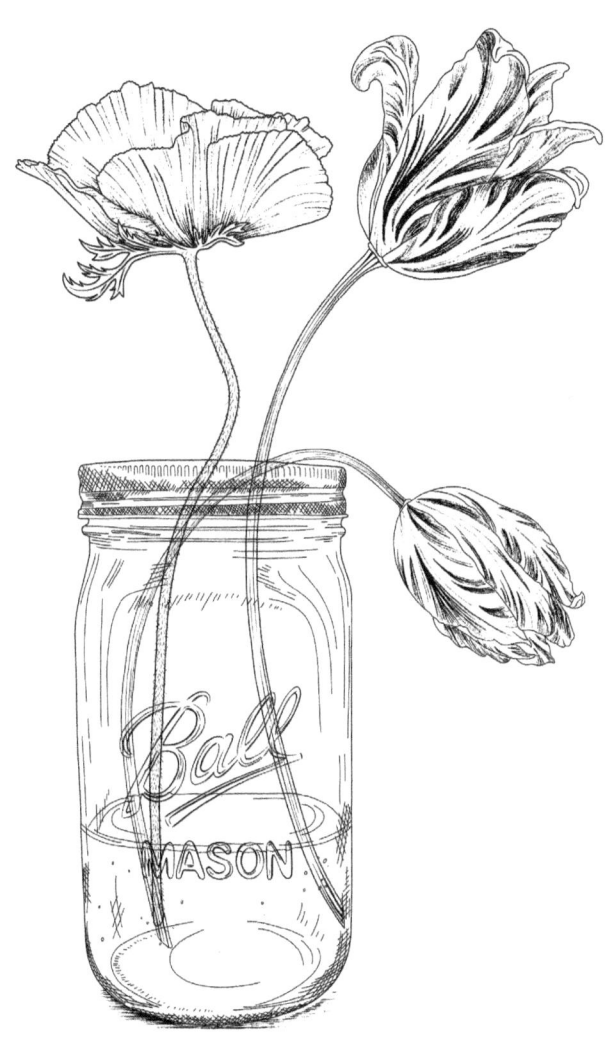

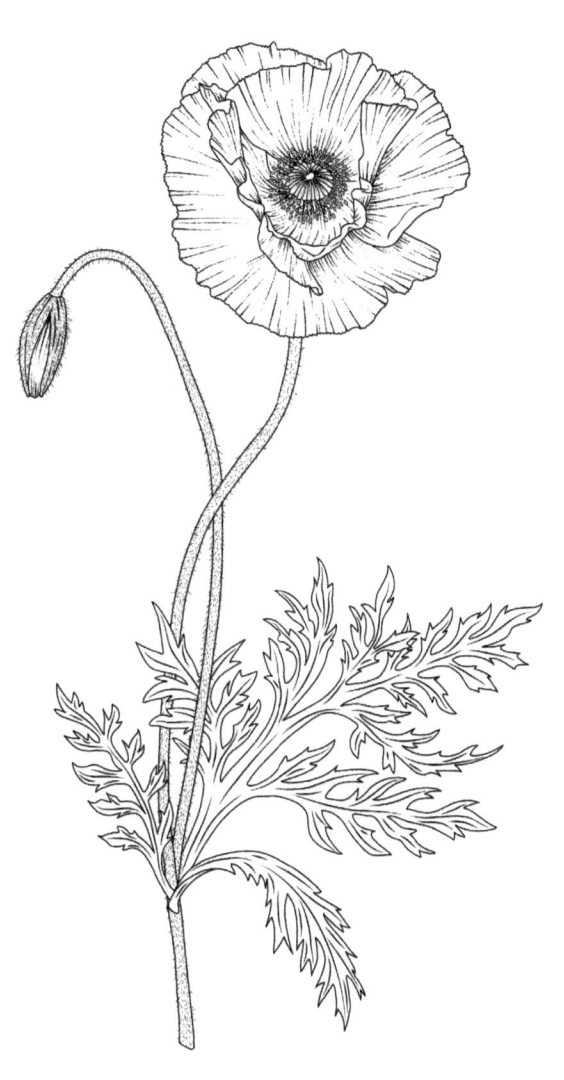

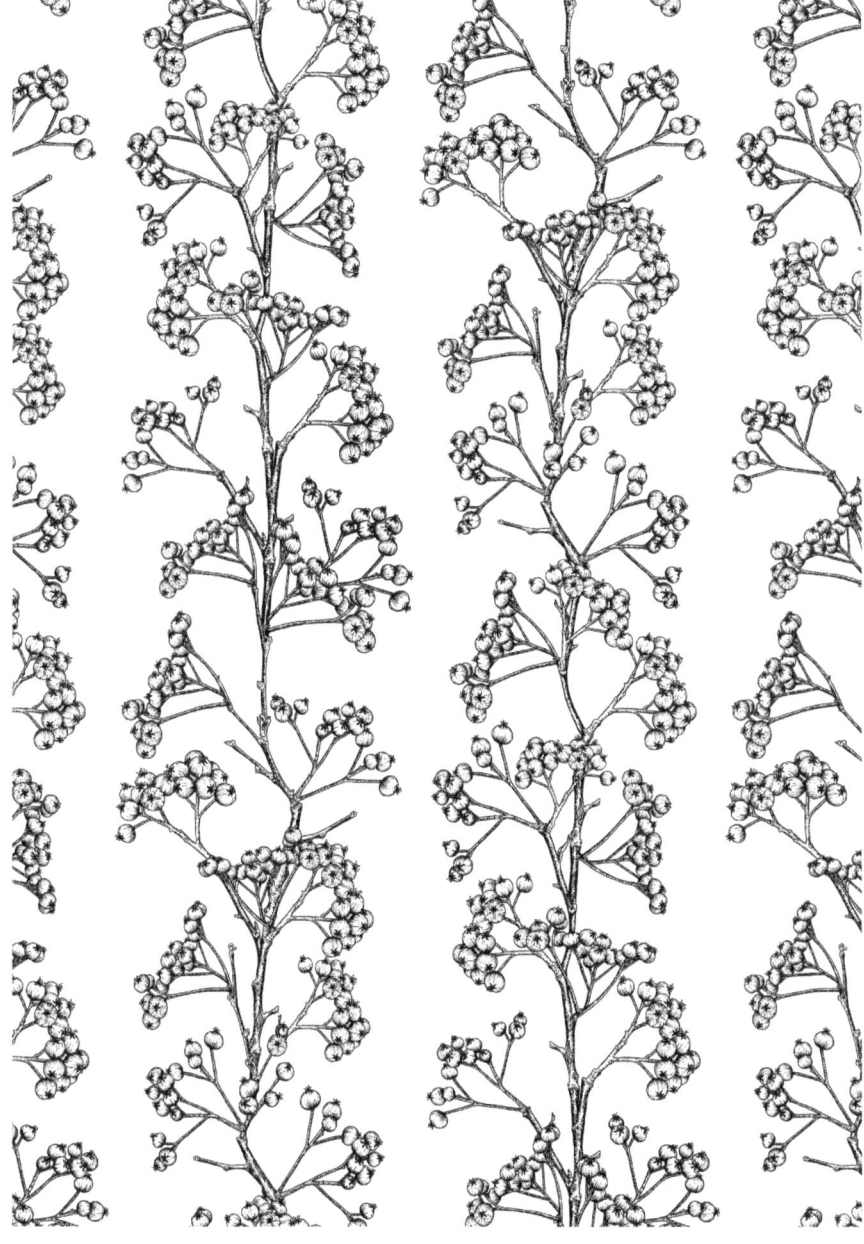

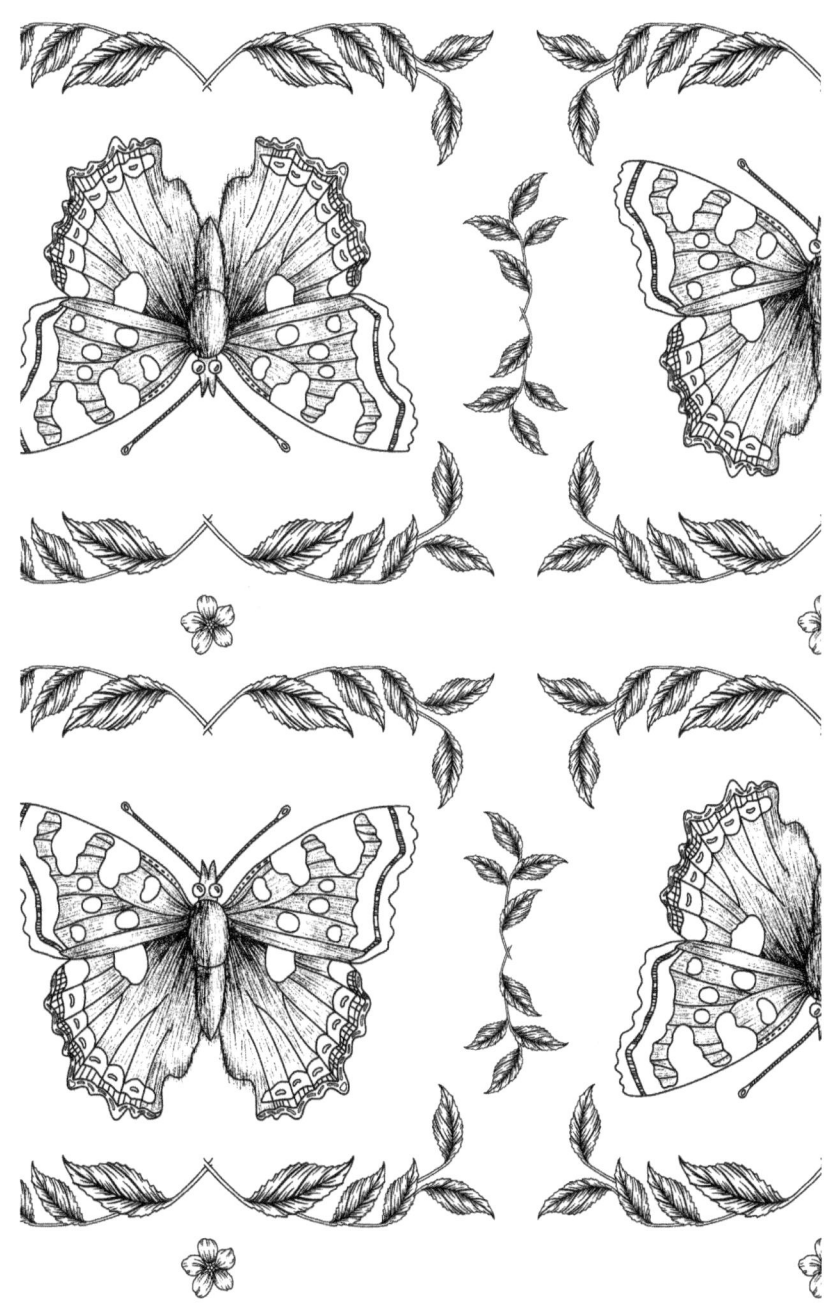

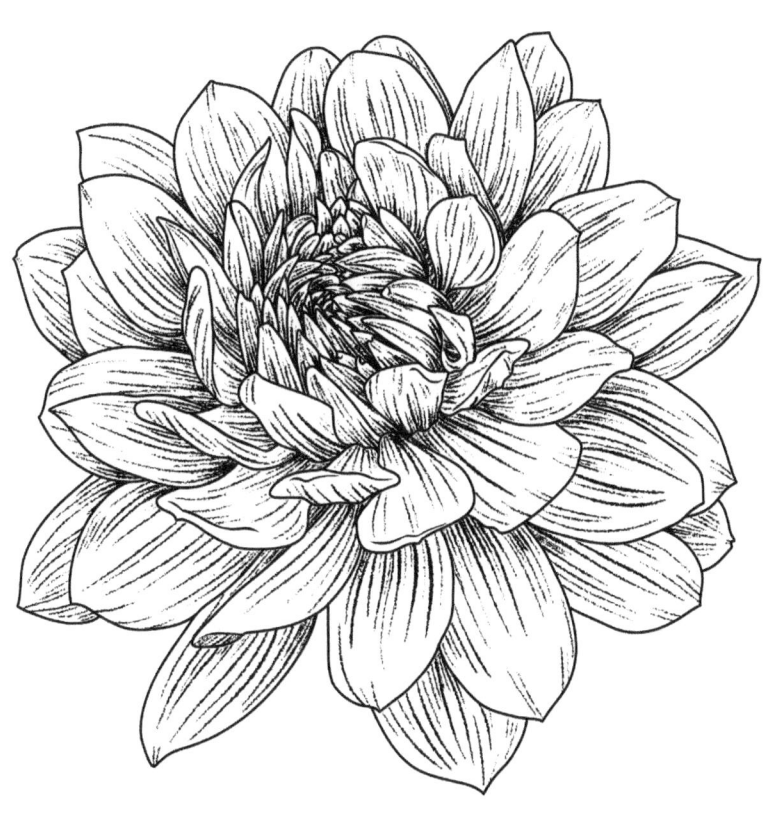

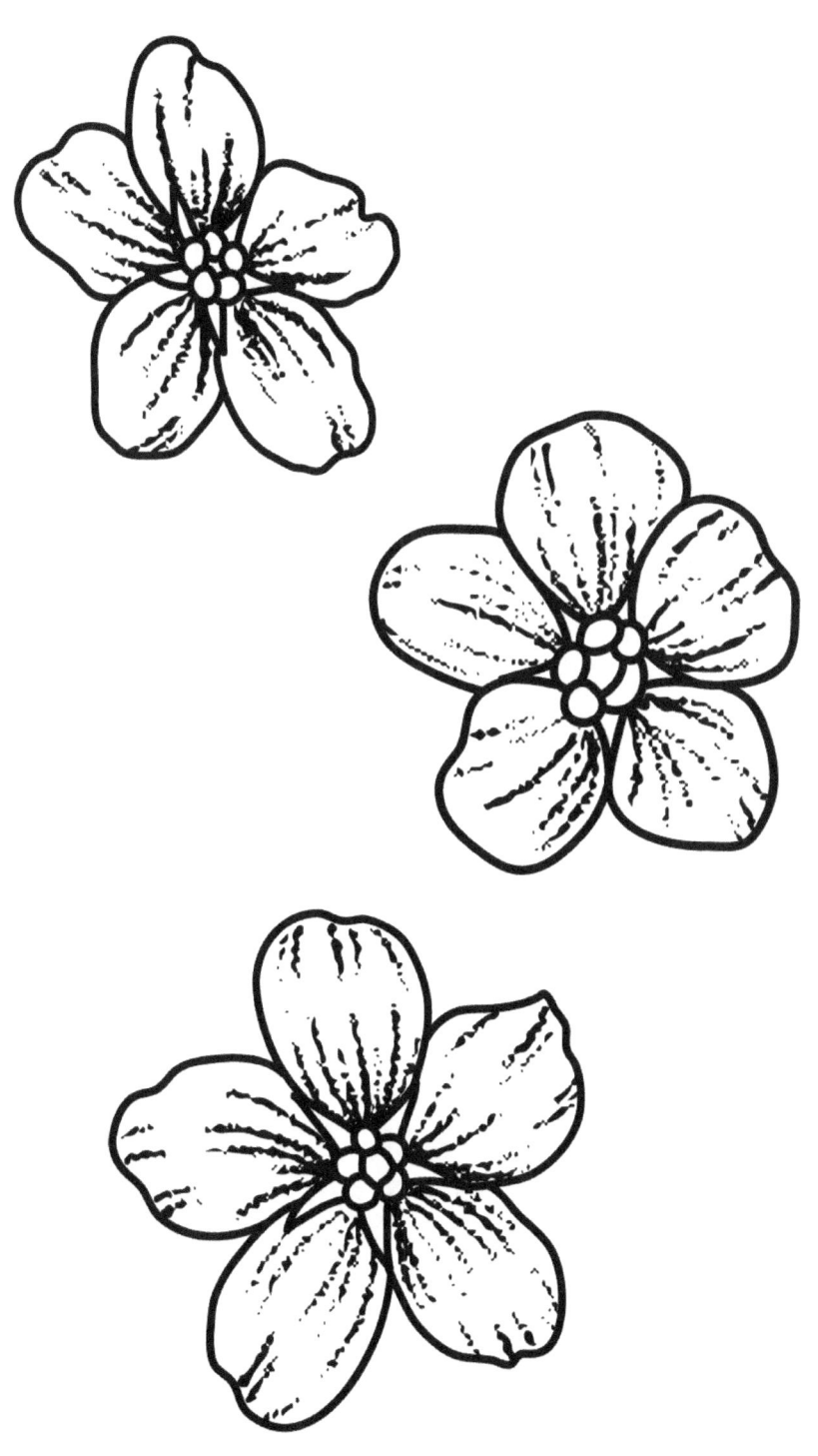

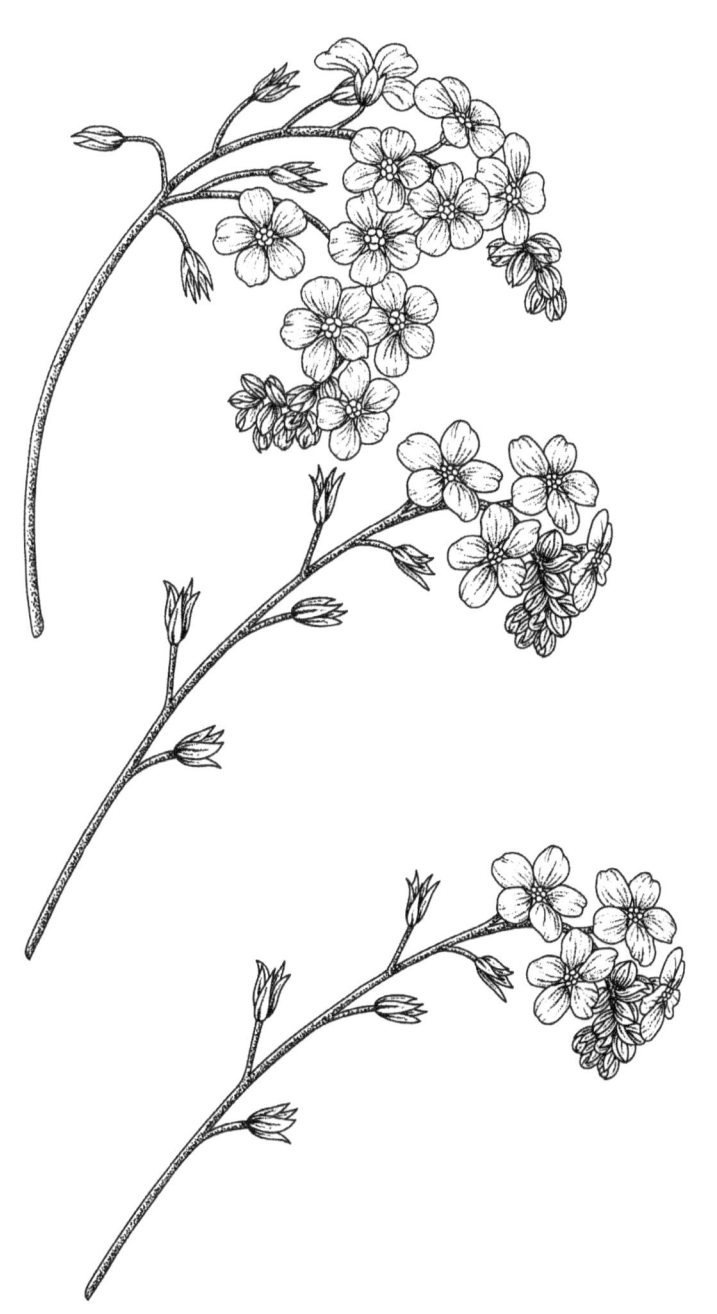

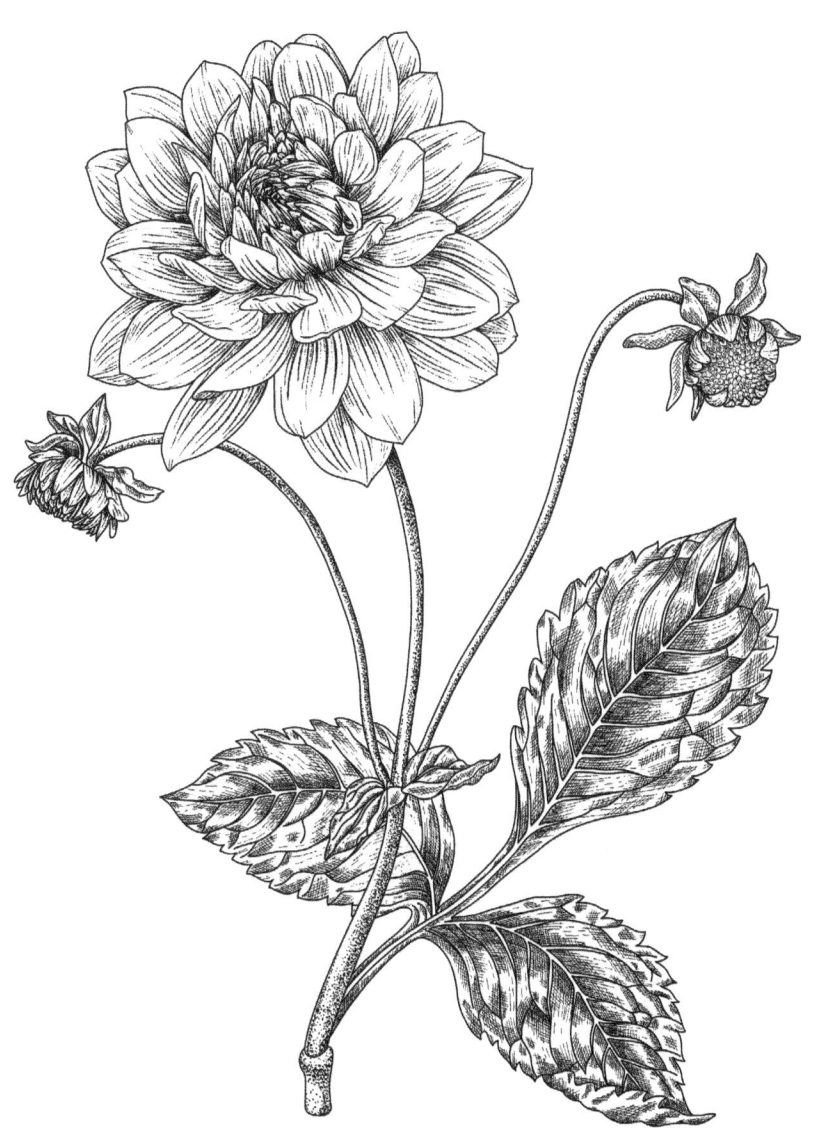

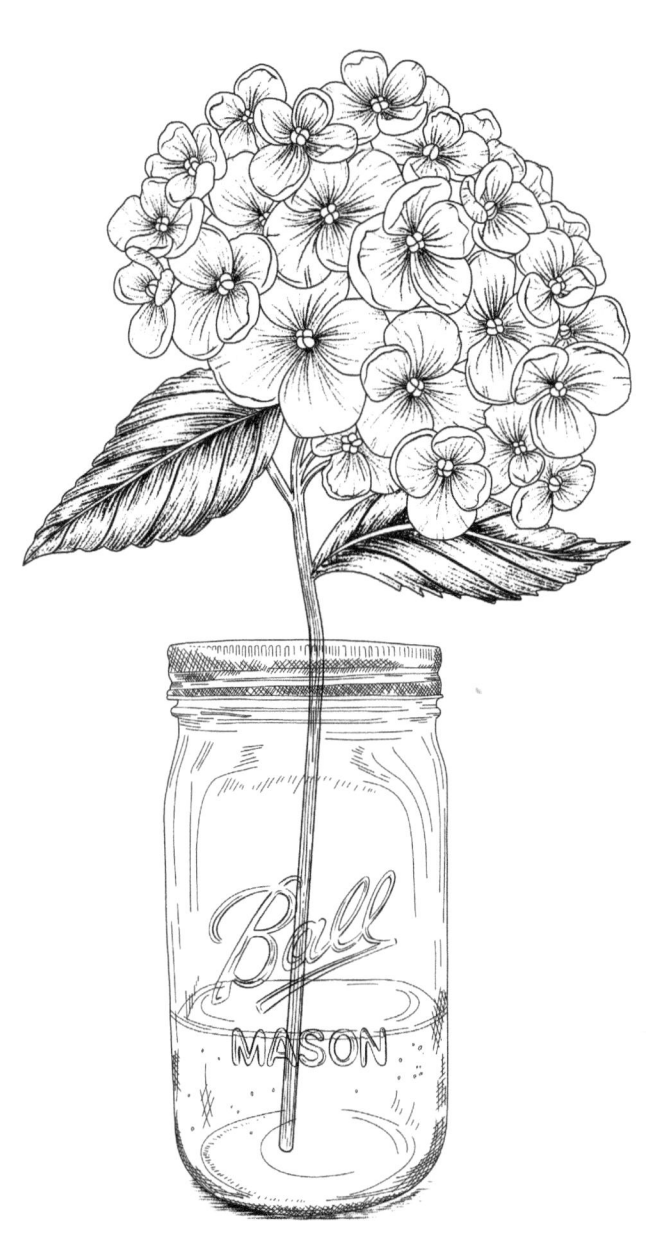

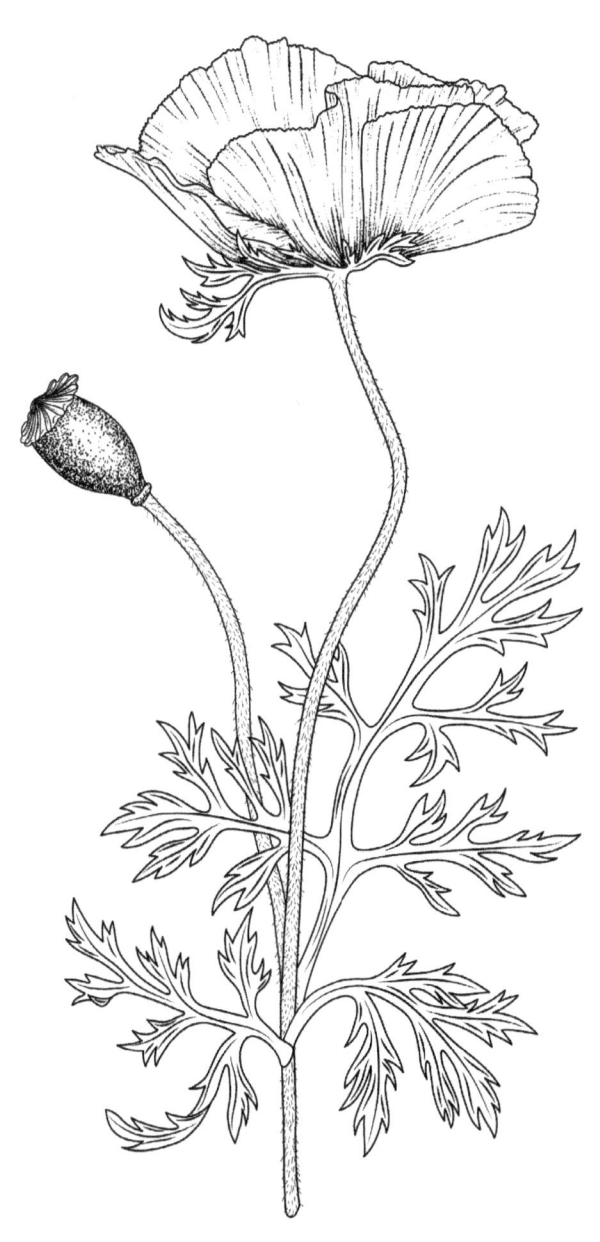

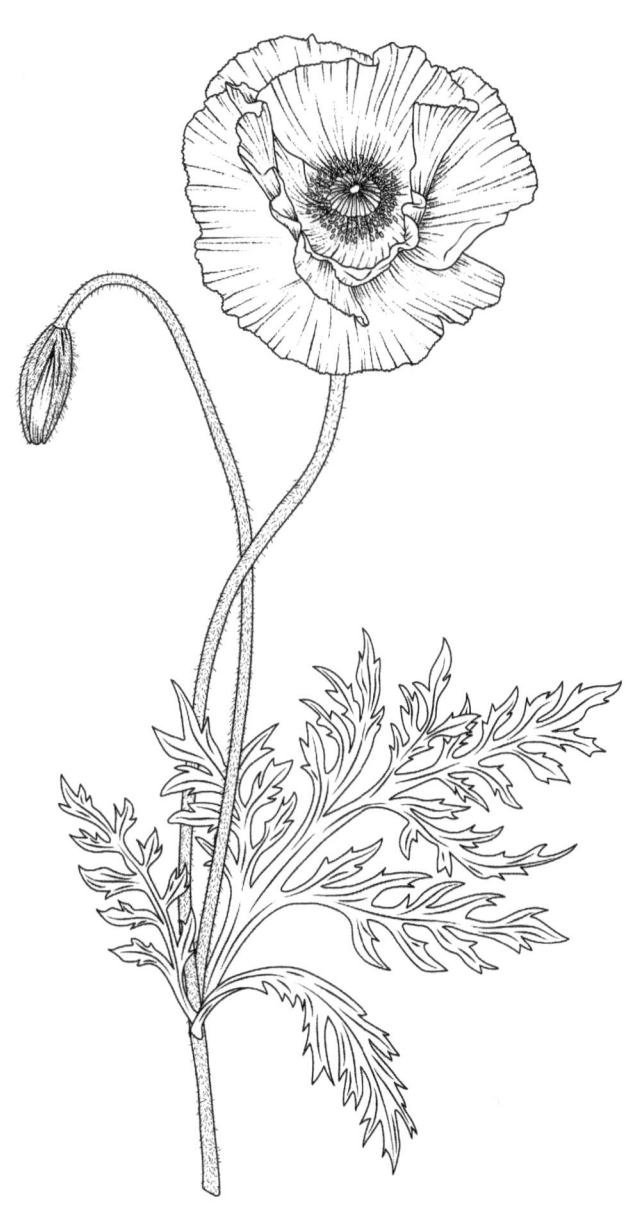

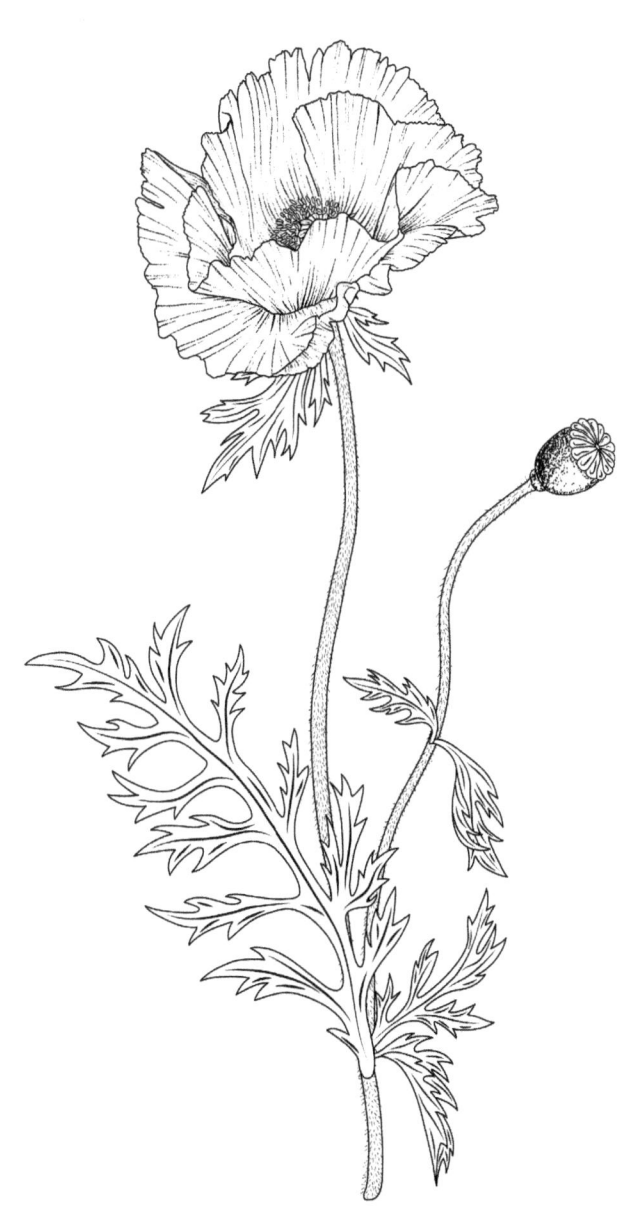

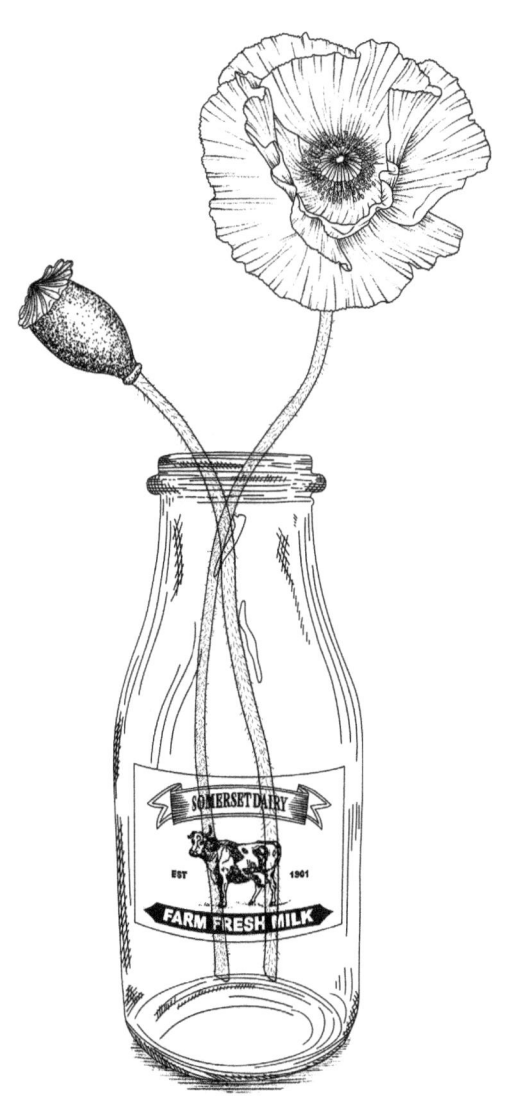

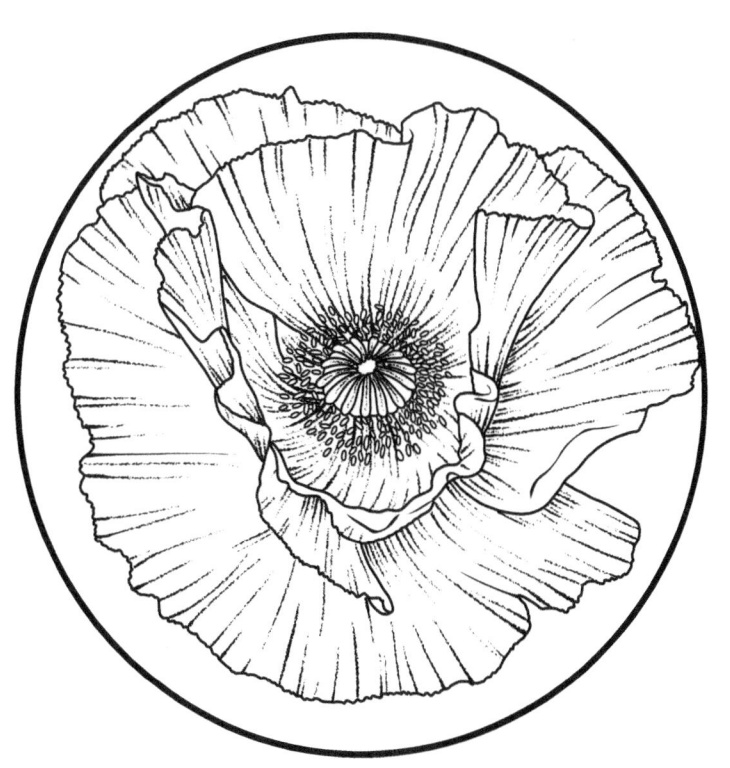

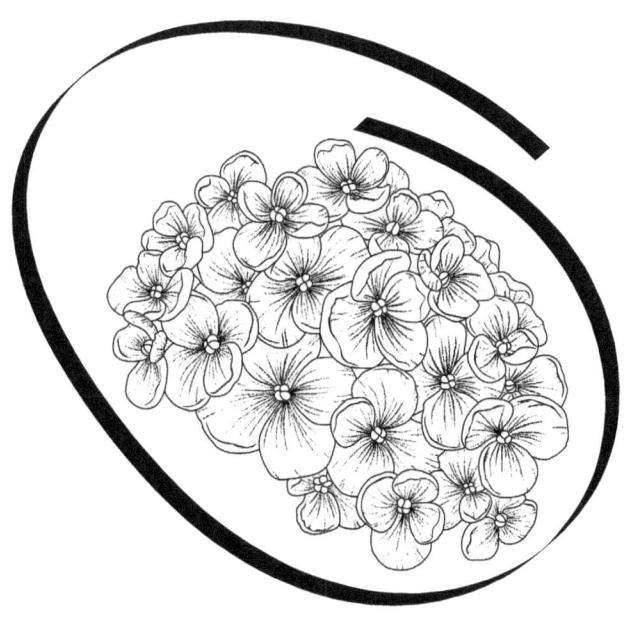

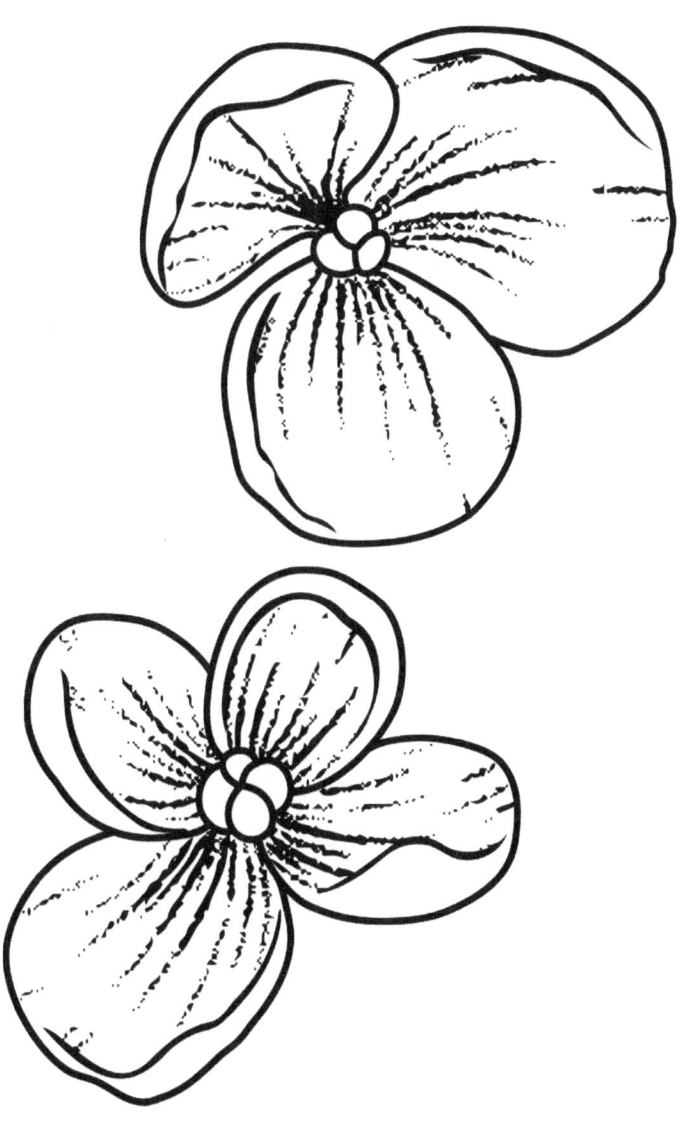

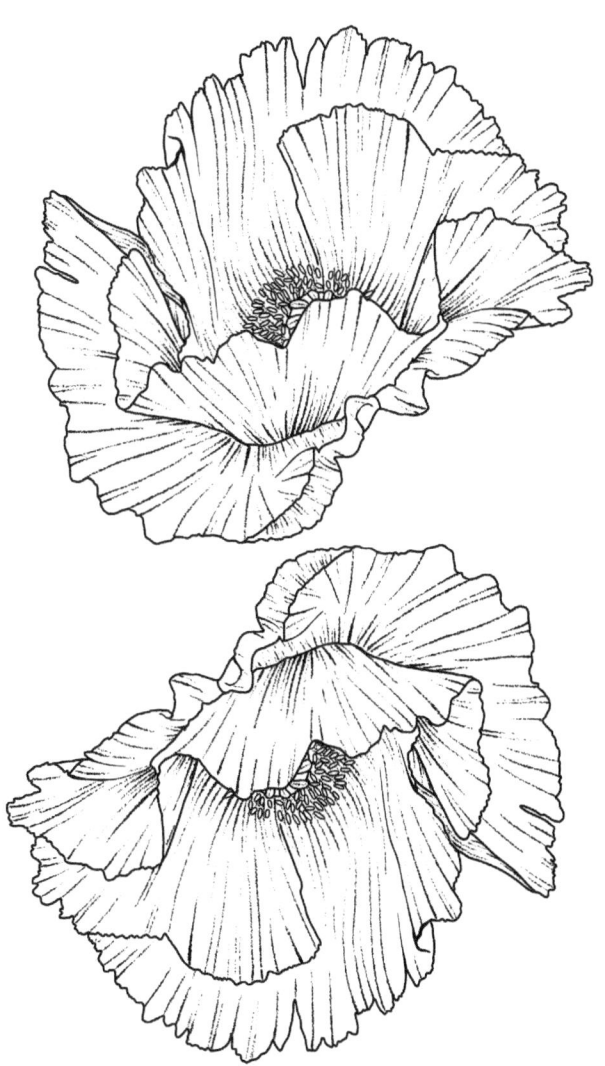

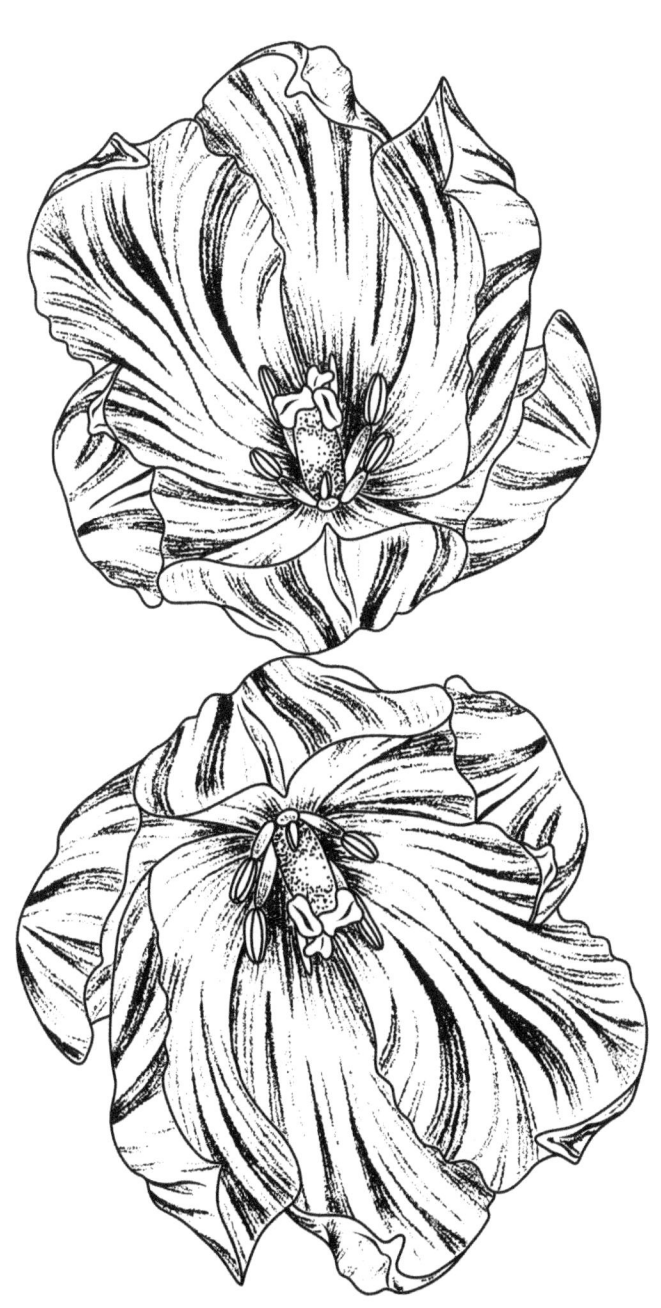

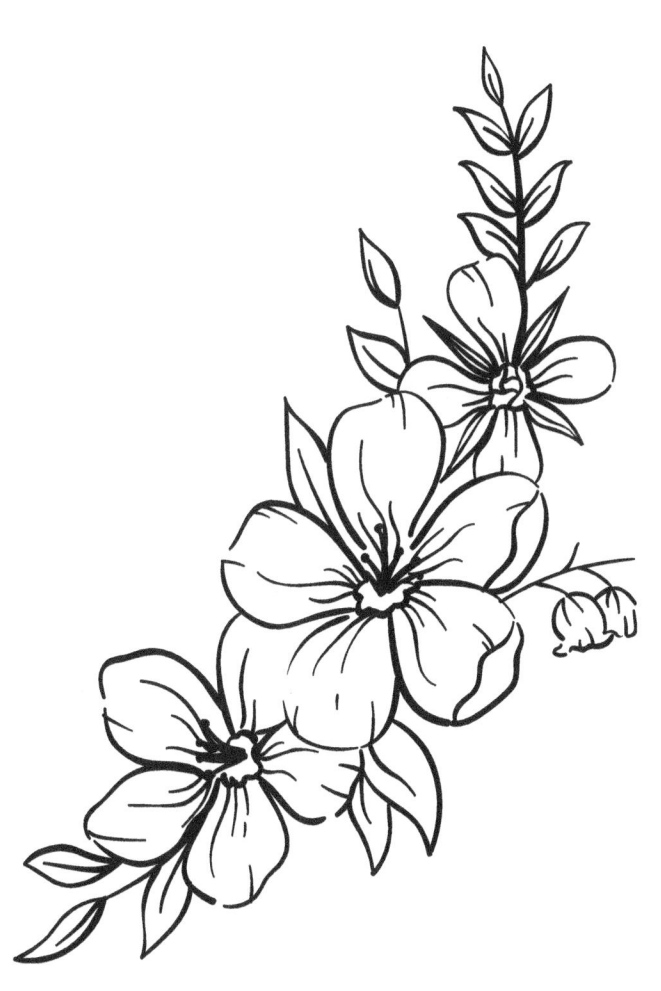

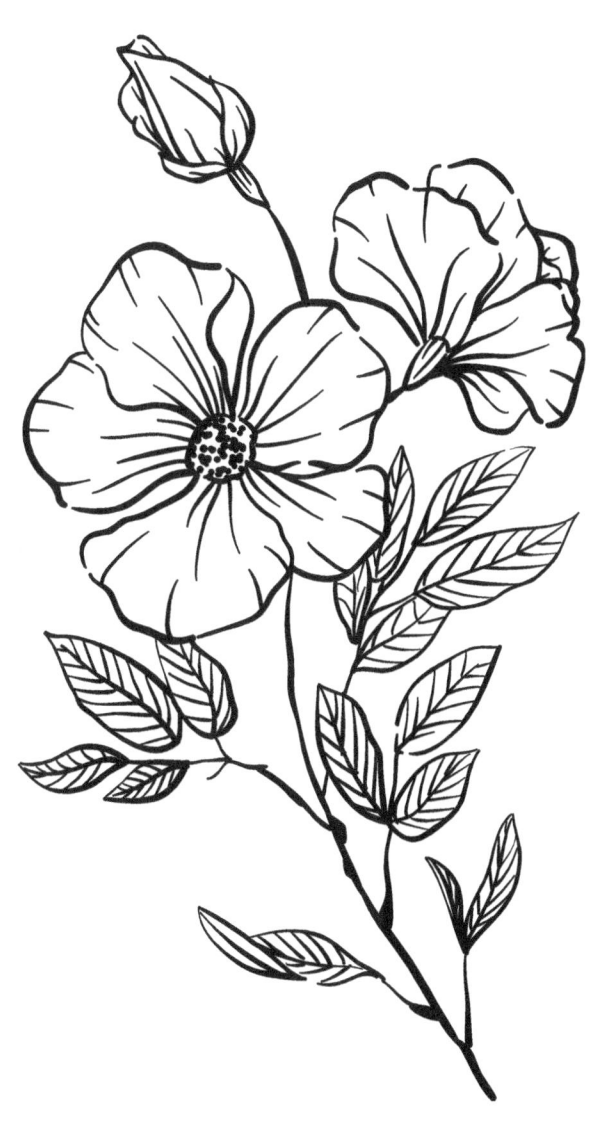

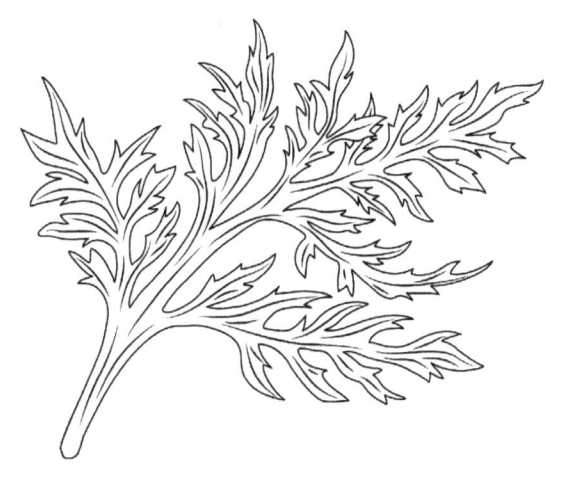
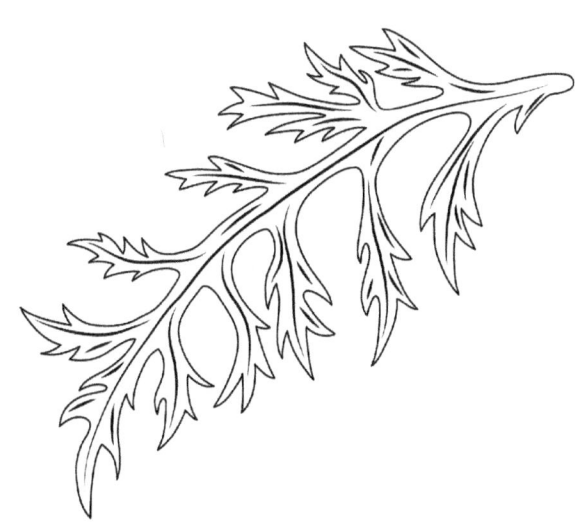

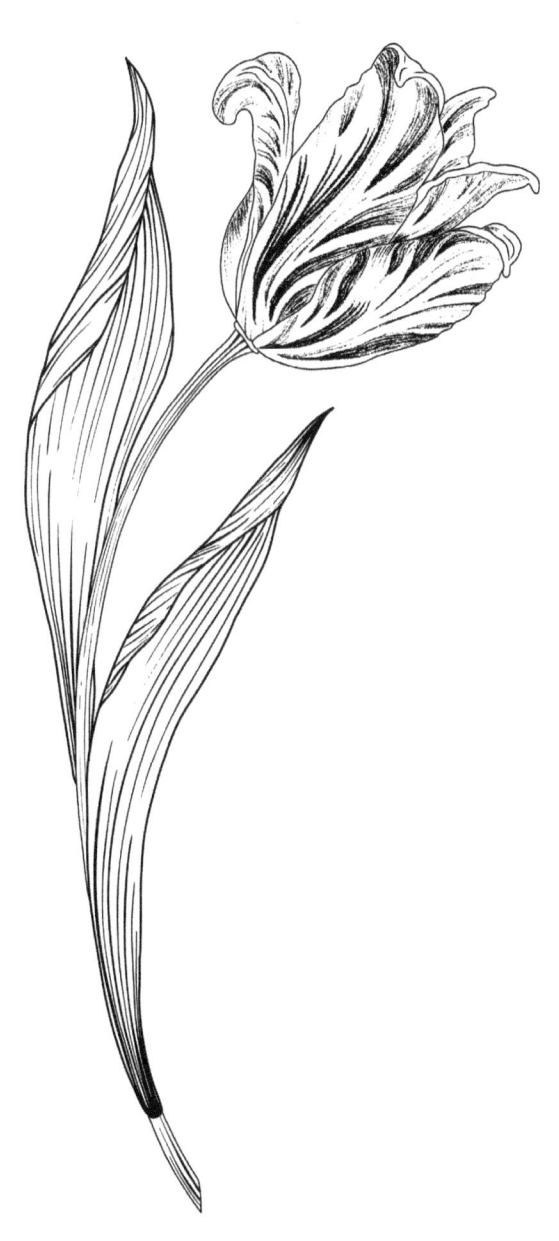

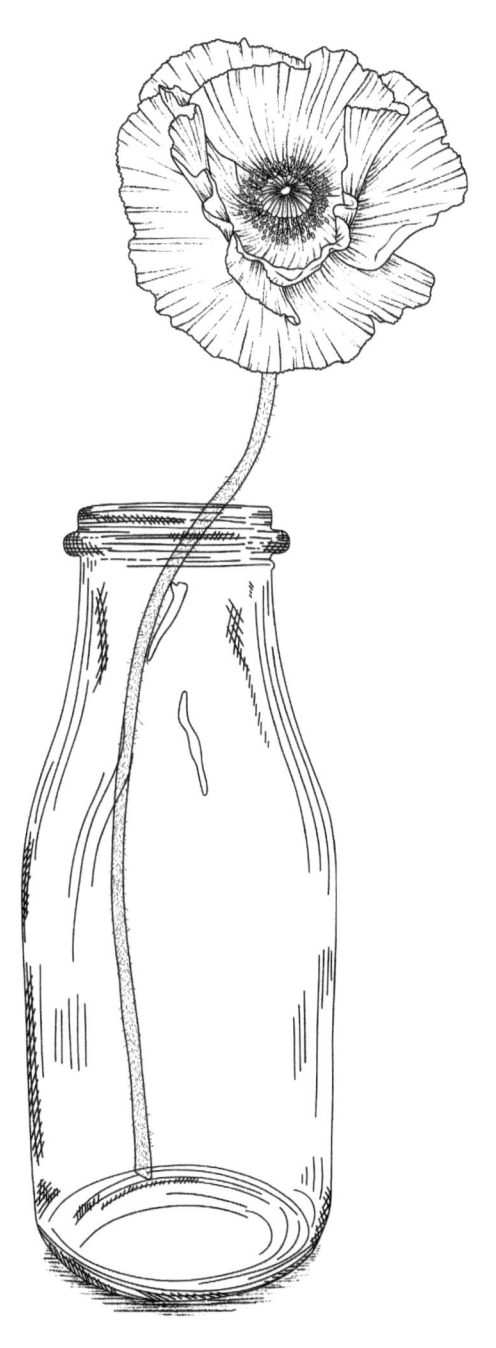

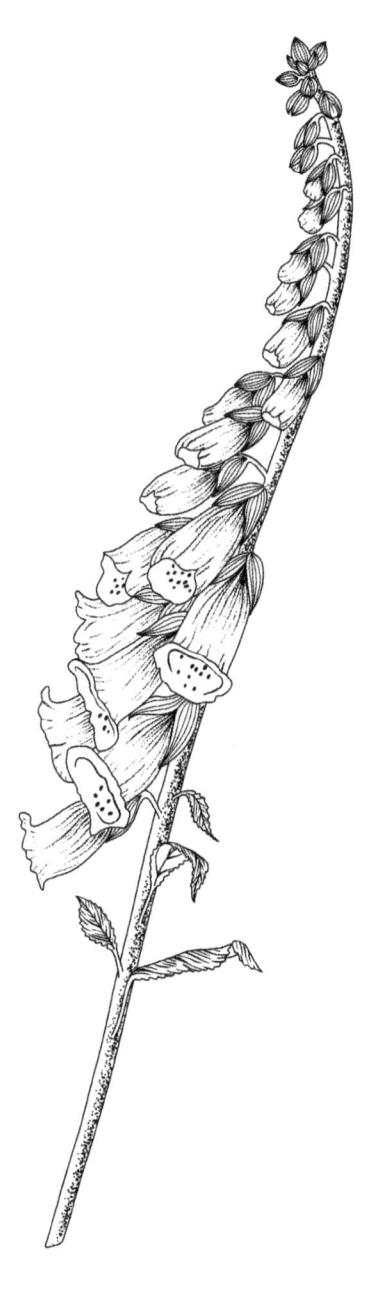

www.ingramcontent.com/pod-product-compliance
Lightning Source LLC
Chambersburg PA
CBHW070335240526
45466CB00027B/2046